Something's Very Wrong

SPORTS PARENTS DRIVE ME NUTS!

TOM GOMES

Visit www.booksurge.com to order additional copies.

To Diane, for proving that love is grand!
To Lindsey, for epitomizing discipline and commitment!
To Tommy, for demonstrating victory through self confidence!
To Alex, for maintaining sanity through a sense of humor!
I love you all, with every beat of my heart!

TABLE OF CONTENTS

Introduction 7

Hooks, Worms & Moby Dick 12

Stripe-aphobia 18

Magic, Legends and Unicorns 22

The Bride of Hitler 26

Those Precious, Family Videos 30

Old Bones and Young Hearts 34

I Hope These Kids Start Losing 38

The Gentle Giant 42

Can He Survive in Society? 48

The Rabid Creature 52

My Foxhole Buddy 56

I'll Never Eat Fried Chicken Again! 60

Kissing Your Belly Button 64

My Daughter the Addict 68

Grampy the Caveman 72

Insanity Vanity Plates 76

The M.I.A. Mom 80

Those Angelic Volunteers 84

Super-Kids? No Thanks! 88

Johnny, the Angel of Death 94

Have You Met Woody Enhard? 100

A M P L I F Y 104

I Failed! I Failed Miserably! 108

Hey Fool! It's Me! 114

Mom? Dad? Can We Talk? 120

Epilogue 124

INTRODUCTION

He killed him. With his bare, bloodied fists one Hockey father mercilessly beat another father to a slow, painful death by robotically pounding him on the side of his head – as nearly a dozen, horrified children watched on in frozen terror. As the national and international media outlets swarmed this small New England town, the entire country soon became saddened and captivated as the details of the story began to unfold. How could this happen? Two average Hockey dads at their sons practice session argue over a play on the ice – leading to this unimaginable outcome. Shocked! Stunned! Surprised! We asked ourselves again and again, how could this happen? If however, you have a child engaged in youth sports, then perhaps your only surprise was that this terrible tragedy didn't happen much sooner and much more often.

An out of control father screaming obscenities at a bewildered fifteen year old umpire? Two mothers screaming at each other just hours before the opening curtain of their daughter's dance recital? A *gotta-win coach* arrogantly defending his actions to bench the nine year old son of an impassioned father because the coach *"needs to win this game"*? These public demonstrations of spastic, out of control adults, happens all too regularly at these children events. Like a prickly weed that snakes itself through a beautiful flower garden, these misfit parents manage to take something that is intended to be fun for the children, and turn it into a stressful, highly emotional, angst filled event for parents and children alike. You know the parent I'm talking about. He lives in every community and he somehow manages to find his way into so many of your child's events. He's rude. He's self centered. He's a know it all. He eats, sleeps and drinks sports. He's loud. He's arrogant. And yes, this is an equal opportunity club and quite often, the he is a she that shares all the same innate qualities with her male counterpart. He's bold. He's pushy. But mostly, he's irritating. Like nails on a blackboard, he sends the hair on your neck running for cover. He's completely capable of catapulting Mother Theresa into a postal episode! For nearly twenty years, I have passionately watched my three children participate in hundreds of athletic events and I have found this inventory of arrogant adult behavior to be simply unlimited.

Look. I'm not going to sit here and expound on all the wonderful values organized, youth sports programs offer our children. If you're kids are enrolled in any activity, then you already know about the benefits of teamwork; the disciplines; the confidence building; the thrill of victory; the agony of defeat, blah, blah, blah. You've heard about, as well as preached these benefits for years. Hey, the fact of the matter is that a very annoying, small percentage of imbeciles are consistently and effectively destroying all these wonderful programs and robbing you and your children of what is rightfully yours. Not only are the sheer numbers of these morons multiplying at an alarming rate, but their individual comments and actions continue to push the envelope well beyond what's publicly acceptable. This asinine behavior includes the verbal abuse of their very own children – the uninhibited humiliation of the volunteer coaching staff – the total disregard for all the parents and children that surround them - and the complete lack of respect for the umpires that by all accounts, are there for one simple reason - to provide balance and keep the children safe.

Just open the newspaper or catch the evening headlines and you know what I'm talking about – *"another out of control parent loses it at junior's game"*. Google up 'sports parents' and you'll get more hits than Babe Ruth in his prime. If you need the visual proof, then execute the same search on Youtube.com and watch these clowns perform their ridiculous acts with your very own eyes. This epidemic is so concerning, that several organizations throughout the country are dedicated to this advocacy mission. For example, the National Alliance for Youth Sports (NAYS) and the Institute for the Study of Youth Sports (ISYS) are staffed with brilliant people doing all the right things to stem the tide. It's getting so bad that in February of 2008, the Massachusetts legislature passed House Bill 4479 that introduces new curriculum to teach sportsmanship, hopefully reducing the volume and intensity of school sports fights. Personally, I think it's terrific that our tax dollars will be spent on teaching kids good sportsmanship. But who the heck is going to teach the parents?

Look. I'm not a legislator. I'm no researcher or therapist. And I'm certainly no doctor. I'm just a dad. A parent who loves his children and a parent, like you, that is completely capable of applying common sense to this madness. And I'm fed up! It's time to bring this garbage out to the curb and dispose of it. It's stinking up everything else that's good with youth sports. So while the doctors and sociologists try to determine therapeutic remedies for these sickies, I thought you and I might have some fun at their expense. I am certain that you will recognize, and I hope that you will enjoy this satirical, short story collection of twenty five misguided parents who are acutely afflicted with the incorrigible plague I humbly refer to as POTT-itis (Parents Over The Top).

HOOKS, WORMS &
MOBY DICK

Something's very wrong I tell you! Something's very wrong! I was robbed. I was swindled in broad daylight. I was mugged while hundreds of people were within the range of my voice. I was pillaged while my three young children looked on helplessly. I didn't lose my wallet. My jewelry was not taken. My new truck was not stolen. Something much more important was ripped from my insides. I was forced to surrender a priceless family moment – a day filled with laughter and joy – to a wildly ignorant man who accused my five year old son of cheating. Cheating – while engaged in the sport of Fishing! That's right – fishing!

Now I will gladly tell you that I didn't know the first thing about fishing then, and I don't know much more about it now. But the one thing I am quite certain – absolutely certain about - is the complete inability for anyone on the planet to cheat in this sport – especially a five year old. My son is not Doctor Doolittle and did not convince the fish to eat his bait. My son did not equip his line with some type of high tech, heat sensing hook (do fish give off heat?). My son did not spend years secretly breeding and nurturing some delicious worm that proves to be irresistible to anything with gills. My son is not a cheat!

I'll start from the beginning! It was a gorgeous spring day and our home town was readying for its annual children's fishing derby. The pond was no larger than a couple of football fields. It was more than adequately stocked just days before with oversize trout and bass that most fishermen would kill for. Food concessions were lining the parking lot. Loud speakers were barking out instructions and hundreds of children escorted by their unfamiliar parents were filing in one after another.

My three children had insisted we arrive nearly two hours before everyone else so we could be assured of a good spot. Equipped with not much more than a few cheap rods I bought at the dollar discount store – no tackle box – a cracked margarine container full of worms I dug up in the back yard the night before – and a cooler packed with juice boxes, candy and toy action figures – we were ready to begin our transformation to fishermen (or fisherpeople for those politically correct readers)!

The first signal of the impending robbery came very early on. As we stood impatiently alone, accompanied only by mosquitoes large enough to be picked up by military radar, the criminal made his initial contact with us. With thousands of feet of barren shoreline to choose from, he opted to set up camp directly abutting us. His excuse? "This is our lucky spot!". One quick glimpse at this guy and you knew immediately that he took this fishing stuff quite seriously. He was adorned in some Gilligan like hat that had more hooks hanging off of it than Wal-Mart had hanging in aisle seventeen. His multi-pocketed vest was covered with lures, colorful flies and what appeared to be some type of blue ribbon award. Attached to his belt was a foldable pair of shiny pliers that I later found out were used to rip out internal fish organs that got in the way of his eighty nine cent fishing hook. Last but not least, strapped tightly around his leg, reflecting the bright morning sun, was an eighteen inch hunting knife - which I'm assuming was there in the unlikely event that the Loch Ness Monster was in fact now hiding in this New Hampshire pond. And his young son was dressed almost identically!

Several hours into this terrific day, fish after fish were being reeled in by dozens of rookie youngsters. Every one of them wishing that it measures as the biggest catch of the day and dreaming that they walk away with the trophy and the grand prize $100 gift certificate to the local toy store. My eight year old son, quite intent on teaching his younger five year old brother a lesson or two managed to catch a couple of throw backs. My eleven year old daughter spent most of the day not fishing and reminding us how *"really yucky gross"* worms were and how sad she felt *"for all the fish in the whole wide world"*. My youngest son, undeterred by all the bravado around him, remained focused on casting his knotted line just five feet away into knee deep water.

Suddenly, we hear commotion from the young and old positioned shoulder to shoulder along the waterfront. Like watching synchronized line dancers in a Broadway show, one person after another gasped loudly, stared in utter amazement, and pointed their determined finger toward the very edge of the water. As the human domino effect quickly moved its way toward our clan, we couldn't believe our eyes. A fifteen inch wide mouth bass was leisurely making his way, uninhibited along the shoreline in no more than eight inches of water. He glided gracefully along, directly under our extended rods. My five year old son, unaware of the euphoric fisherpeople, innocently reeled in his bait-less line, and conveniently hooked this Moby Dick look alike through the side of his slimy, gilled body. At which point I quickly reached down and pulled the fish out of the water with my bare hands! The crowd went crazy with applause and even crazier with laughter. While my family and pond full of new friends were elated, my well dressed neighbor to the left of us was little amused.

As the event approached its close, the event coordinator announced the winner over the loud speaker system. Moby Dick and his unorthodox capture (and immediate subsequent release) won the grand prize for my son! None of us could believe our luck as stranger after stranger came over to genuinely congratulate my very proud, five year old hero.

Life couldn't get any better that day – but it certainly could get worse - as our neighbor fisherman was willing to prove. Within seconds after the ceremony had completed, this numbskull had trounced to the judges to lodge his formal complaint. His boisterous comments included ridiculous verbs and adjectives such as *"unfair"* or *"shouldn't count"* or *"cheating"* or *"broke the rules"*. (Is there actually a book of rules somewhere for town fishing tournaments?) Any observing adult in the crowd knew that this guy was thirty cards short of a full deck. Every adult knew that—but not my five year old who couldn't help but hear every word. As his eyes began to tear up, I did the only thing I could do. We took our awards, we thanked the judges, and we proudly walked back to our vehicle while leaving the bumbling fool and the begrudging judges in their heated discussion.

Later that night, we celebrated the victory with cake, ice cream and a flood of kind and encouraging words to all of our children. As we put them to bed that night, we knew that their first lessons on adult jealousy and the adult extreme competitive nature would unfortunately, not be their last lesson. Something's very wrong I tell you! Something's very wrong!

STRIPE-APHOBIA

Something's very wrong I tell you! Something's very wrong. What is it that compels a grown man to lose total control of his common sense? To purge himself of every manner learned, and to have a complete absence of any ability to think logically? What is it that compels this nincompoop to disrespect every women, child and adult in a fifty-yard radius? The answer? The answer is more shocking than his behavior! A bad call from a referee - a bad call from a thirteen year old referee!

Now you would think that just being outside on the first sunny, weekend in months would be relaxing. You would think that watching your child get some exercise and having some fun would be enjoyable. You would think that your son's team ahead by five points – at half time - in a soccer game - is calming. But nnoooo! Not for this doofus!

So there they stood. Parents from both teams gathered on the sidelines. Some sitting. Some standing. Some cheering sounds of encouragement toward their offspring. Some barely watching while catching up with an old friend. In the shadows, pacing back and forth several yards away from the other parents stood an exiled, tall, lonely man. His six foot framed, two hundred plus pound body was wrapped in a vinyl jacket adorning a Pro Football logo across the back. A colorful visor cap displayed his favorite Pro Hockey team, as he stood next to his Sports Illustrated folding chair. And where was this man's loving wife and daughter? Incognito! Protecting themselves from what they predicted was certain to happen.

Twenty-two young children were on the field – all pretending to know what they're doing in this game of soccer. Some kids were laughing while others were intent on being the hero. Some kids were tying their shoelaces (again!) or picking dandelions from the un-mowed grass while others were blowing kisses to their attentive Moms. All in all, it was a perfect day – until, until 'the penalty'! The legend says - that it was in fact, a bad call. A boy from the losing team had inadvertently tripped one of the players from the winning team, while he was on a breakaway – heading towards what might have been yet another goal. The Referee, a thirteen year old, hard working kid, had blown his whistle - while the fool of a father on the sidelines had blown his temper.

As the Ref shouted out the penalty, the oxygen barely escaping from his young lungs, the Boogieman bellowed back, "Are you out of your F'ing mind!!?". All of the laughter and conversation came to an instantaneous, frightening halt! Twenty one of the twenty two kids watched in fright as the Boogieman marched passionately onto the field, while one desperate child, simply sat down, stared at the ground, almost anticipating the next few minutes. Mrs. Boogieman, held her head in her hands, and appeared to be praying for a 'Witness Protection Program for Idiot Husbands'. The remarkable, volunteer coaches, as well as some other parents from both teams, brought the situation quickly under control, as if rehearsed and planned for. But the damage had been done! The event was ruined. The children were shocked and the child-referee was simply mortified.

Less than an hour later, at the Ice Cream stand, life was back to normal for nearly everyone. The brainless Father? He was later diagnosed as a Type 1 Stripe-aphobic. Stipe-aphobia is a growing disease affecting middle-aged men, more commonly

X-jocks who are trying to live their lives through the eyes of their sons. Over exposure to black and white stripes, usually in a vertical pattern, and occasionally found on some referee shirts, have been known to trigger this uncontrollable, ignorant and irrational behavior.

While Stripe-aphobia is not at epidemic proportions yet, it is growing at an alarming rate with case after case being reported throughout the country. Professionals are unanimous in their treatment of this disease. If you feel you are ever suffering from these symptoms, simply repeat to yourself, quietly, ten times.... *"It's all about the kids! It's all about the kids!"*. A simple treatment for such a dramatic illness – yet few chose to even try it! Something's very wrong I tell you! Something's very wrong!

MAGIC, LEGENDS & UNICORNS

Something's very wrong I tell you! Something's very wrong! Why don't most people understand my true potential? I've been a hockey stick my whole life. I've been sitting patiently in this Sporting Goods store just waiting for only the right person to buy me. Not just any person, but the right person. You see, I am an upper class hockey stick. The price tag adorning my long slim body is usually printed with a very large number. The player who can afford me will undoubtedly improve his game. Why the mere mention of my brand name demands attention from even the most novice player. Simply holding me in your hands will improve your skills five fold as I will do all the work - and you the player - will need to do nothing.

Who will be my lucky owner? I can usually spot that perfect person from a mile away. See that lady standing in the sneaker aisle with her teenage son? She's definitely not the right person. How could she possibly allow her son to wear sneakers with no logos? She's too practical for me? So how about that jock in aisle six? See him holding up that stack of coupons trying to find the baseball glove that's on sale? No owner of mine would ever buy anything on sale! And see the guy who just threw me back on the shelf. He doesn't believe in my magical powers! He probably doesn't believe in the tooth fairy either. I'm glad he put me back up here. Phew!

And how about - - - -. Wait! Here he is. Here's my new owner. I'm sure of it. He was in here just last week and bought all of my second and third cousins – the whole family. He bought the finest and most expensive set of golf clubs ever manufactured. I overheard him tell the salesperson that he was beginning his very first golf lesson the next day and he was certainly '*gonna kick some butt*'. Now here's a guy who knows what I'm talking about! And this must be his lovely wife and daughter behind him. Mom? Sis? Dad? Ahhh, my new family!

Like spotting a red rose amongst weeds; without hesitation he plucked me from my cold, steel shelf and began comforting me with his kind words. "*Oh yah, this is the baby. This is the one we need.*" Obviously, he was an incredibly brilliant man! As he handed me off to his nine year old daughter, her eyes lit up with joy. We immediately bonded. Dad, Sis and I knew at that very moment that she was now about to become the youngest female to ever play in the all-male, National Hockey League. All she needed was me!

The ride to my new home was awesome! It was my first time ever in a fancy new sports car. I think that whole theory about the guy, who drives a fancy sports car because he's overcompensating for shortcomings elsewhere in his personal life, is just simply not true. Dad's just a guy who likes the finer things in life! I thought I had finally made it. Like all my relatives before me I had hit the big time. But quickly, things began to fall apart. As soon as we arrived home I was tossed into the bucket with all the old hockey sticks – the wooden ones – the cheap ones! Eww! I felt so dirty. The next morning got worse. Sis decided to practice her slap shots. With medium sized rocks lined up along the driveway she hopped from one to another, slamming my beautiful blade along the coarse, black asphalt, pounding my face into the rocks. Later that night, when we showed up at her game she didn't even introduce me to her locker room teammates. No one recognized me. No one cared that I was there. It was devastating.

If this wasn't bad enough, tragedy struck within just a minute or two of the games official start. I lost my magical powers. I couldn't help Sis at all! She couldn't stick handle very well. Her shots on the net were missing by a mile. And every time she passed the puck she didn't come close to hitting her target. I had heard similar stories while growing up in my tiny village. The urban legends that talked about average players who could not be improved, even with our most powerful magic. As the game finished with yet another loss to Sis' team, we left the locker room heading solemnly to the group of waiting parents. I felt horrible. How could I explain this phenomenon? If I couldn't help Sis' game improve, then what was my purpose? Why was I here? Dad quickly approached Sis, grabbing the stick from her hand and forgetting to pass on words of comfort to his discouraged daughter. I was certain I was headed for the big dumpster in the sky. Shockingly, with a wide smile on his face, he walked me into the circle of Dads who begrudgingly made room for us. He proudly went onto boast about my qualifications. How I'm manufactured. How expensive I am. How I am above and beyond all other sticks in the world.

And just then, it became crystal clear. I knew my purpose. The urban legends were true. All of them. I was placed on this earth for bragging rights. No magic. No powers. No abilities. Just bragging rights! Something's very wrong I tell you! Something's very wrong!

THE BRIDE OF HITLER

Something's very wrong I tell you! Something's very wrong! Now there are just certain things that you don't say to a teenager. You don't tell them that drugs are cool! You don't remind them about the huge zit on their forehead. You don't tell them that quitting high school is an option. And you certainly don't tell a room full of vulnerable, teenage girls dressed in spandex and workout clothes that they are *"miserably fat"*.

Now before I get into the story, I will remind you that I've never met a volunteer coach that didn't have my deepest respect. Any adult who wants to volunteer their time to teach and entertain my child earns and deserves that at a minimum. However, when I have to pay, and pay quite generously, for that coaching and training, then all bets are off! My daughter has been dancing since she was old enough to walk. She's very good at it and most importantly, when she is performing, she has a smile on her face that lights up the entire room. And, as you would imagine, the level of competition over these years has heightened at a feverish rate. I support competition. I support motivating these athletes to reach down inside and get to the next level. I support the joy of winning and the glow of a platinum medal in this sport. I think that a coach/teacher that can drive a team toward these accomplishments deserves to be heralded as a winner. But I also think that there are boundaries – undisputable boundaries. And it is the moral responsibility of these adult coaches, these adults that play such an influential role in molding our child's beliefs and values, to never, never extend beyond those boundaries. Never!

So once upon a time there was a room full of twenty eight, anxious and very beautiful teenage girls. They came in all different shapes, sizes and skill levels, but the one thing they shared in common was their love for dance. They could do it all day long – for fun, for fitness or for flattery. This particular day was the first full dress rehearsal for the big show that was only a couple of weeks away. The instructor, who was also the owner of the studio, was in an irritable mood from the moment she entered the building. Even when she was in the best of moods, it involved her usually singling out at least one dancer with barking and chiding comments. But today, she was in an all new zone and was about to reach an all time low. After months of rehearsal with each dancer completely absorbed in her very unique steps, jumps, splits and pirouettes; the instructor decided to move five of the dancers to different positions – thoroughly confusing the entire troupe.

Experience has taught these young ladies to NEVER ask their Nazi-instructor why? So instead, they adjusted as best they could amidst their obvious confusion. Needless to say, the next few rehearsals were frustrating and exhausting. Finally, one brave teen, at the end of rehearsal, opted to step forward and ask about these last minute changes. She was one of the five teens that was moved in the rotation. The instructor's response stunned the room. *"Cuz you are fat! You look miserably fat in these costumes and I want all the fat girls in the back of the stage, away from the audience".*

As you would imagine, over the next several days parents lined up waiting to speak with the bride of Hitler - myself included. I released on her, a blinding barrage of pent up personal frustrations that detailed her historical verbal and social abuse of these children. Over the years I have willingly paid thousands and thousands of dollars for professional dance lessons for my darling princess. And it has been worth every cent to bring that priceless smile to my little girls face. But today, that effervescent smile was erased and replaced with a hurt that will remain unknown and unmeasured for years to come. Something's very wrong I tell you! Something's very wrong!

THOSE PRECIOUS, FAMILY VIDEOS

Something's very wrong I tell you! Something's very wrong! Why is it that we usually never have a camera available, or at least a camera that's turned on, when our kids surprise us with that spontaneous, priceless memory? How we long for that perfect, still image to add to the family collage hanging in the hallway, or a funny video clip that we can play over and over again at the Holiday family gatherings. So many parents have a long list of these wonderful, lost opportunities. The frustration of missing that once in a lifetime perfect shot can be quite painful. Every family I know has experienced this disappointment. Well, almost every family!

Enter the Kodak family. (The names were changed to protect the ignorant). As the first game of the season was about to begin, the moms and dads quickly found their spots in the bleachers that offered the best vantage point. I found the perfect seat that would empower me to cheer encouragements to my offspring. A seat located next to some good friends - while also being far enough away from 'the crazy parents'. The only problem with my seat, as I was soon to find out, was the two empty seats right next to me. While they remained empty for the first half of the game, they were soon filled with the most dangerous of all the idiot parents that I have yet to meet – the 'closet idiot'. Like an alcoholic who denies he has a problem, the closet-idiot publicly admonishes other overzealous parents at the game, but then secretly returns to the security of his suburban home and begins the private, overpowering assault on his own child.

Mr. Kodak seemed nice enough at the onset while Mrs. Kodak was just too quiet to tell. Comfortable small talk about numerous topics allowed many of us to mistakenly judge Mr. Kodak as one of the good guys. His conversation, quick wit and sense of humor never missed a beat, while all the time being attentive to the meticulous videotaping of his daughter's performance throughout the game. I was actually, somewhat proud of Mr. Kodak. I admired his dedication capturing those memories of his daughters' first game of the season.

Now, it wasn't up until about the fourth or fifth game that I began to realize the malignant nature of Mr. Kodak's disease. I noticed him in the corner of the building, standing alone on top of a very large stack of folding chairs. He was balancing on one foot with one stiff arm lodged against the wall, while carefully videotaping with the other arm. Wow! Here was a man completely dedicated to the preservation of those family memories – at any costs! As I approached to see if I could assist him in some way, I caught him narrating live commentary into the video barking out coaching commands and identifying what his precious daughter was doing wrong throughout the game. It hit me like a trailer full of pianos. These were no family videos – they were training videos. Videos that would be fast forwarded and rewound again and again until his starry eyed daughter showed some sign of forgiveness for her lack of effort or skill. This poor little girl!

While I enjoyed the fleeting thought of kicking out the stacked chairs from underneath him, I quickly returned to my gentler side with a fake smile and the nod of my head. I got a quick *"Hey Buddy! You're son's playing a great game, huh?"*. I responded with *"Oh thanks!"*. As I walked away I wondered how different the game looked the second time you watched it, then the third time, the fourth time, the fifth. Oh my, that poor family! I wonder if this closet-idiot spends as much time with his kids on other matters, other matters of a bit more importance? How about videotaping his son's Science project? Creating funny flash cards for his daughter's upcoming Math test? Volunteering the family at the local homeless shelter?

I only hope that I have a camera available on the highly inevitable day when his daughter finally snaps and turns to him in the middle of a critical game and says, *"Dad, I hate this sport! I've always hated this sport! I QUIT!"*. Something's very wrong I tell you! Something's very wrong!

OLD BONES &
YOUNG HEARTS

Something's very wrong I tell you! Something's very wrong! When is it absolutely acceptable for a Dad to NOT participate in a sport with his young son? Answer: When that sport is extreme skateboarding! There are just some sports activities that are much better left to the young at heart – and more importantly the young bones. Now don't get me wrong. There is nothing better in life than spending a Sunday afternoon throwing the football around with my boys – tossing hoops with my daughter – or kicking the soccer ball around with all three of them. Those times are precious, the memories are priceless and the fresh air and exercise is invaluable. As a matter of fact, I'm usually the one instigating the activities. I'm also, almost always the one that gets injured first. Whether it's a basketball that forced my finger to bend the wrong way, a football thrown too early that landed square in the back of my skull or a soccer ball kicked fiercely and directly into my groin. Regardless of the embarrassing pains, I return every weekend to anxiously start the process all over again. However, there is a bold line that I will draw and that usually begins with anything that requires me to cautiously and meticulously balance this experienced, old body of mine on tiny little wheels rolling at excessive speeds down wooden ramps with eight foot vertical drops. No mature, responsible man should be too proud to tell his children that he's not ready to learn this sport now or at any time in the immediate future.

Unfortunately, not all dads share my wisdom. Enter the neighbor. Ron is a terrific dad who is totally committed to his eleven year old son. He is also a dad who is overweight, bald, and out of shape who can't even balance his checkbook, never mind his pear-shaped physique. Ron spent an afternoon at the sporting goods store becoming fully equipped with as many pads, cushions and braces as possible to protect his forty something year old body. Just throw a pair of baggy pants on him that exposes his butt crack—a tee shirt adorned with an unfamiliar logo and profanity—wrap a bandana around his forehead—and he's ready to be called a "boarder"!

His initial training took place on the street in front of our homes. Coached anxiously by his semi-expert son, Ron quickly learned the meaning of 'training ground'. He was up and down and up more often then bowling pins on a league night. As I and the other neighbors thoroughly enjoyed the show, Ron managed to come away unscathed and unbroken by his newfound skill. As he rolled toward the highly entertained spectators lined up on the sidewalk, he proudly informed all of us that he was *"now ready"*, and would be joining his son at the indoor skate park the next day. A pack of wild dogs could not keep me from missing this spectacle.

The skate park was enormous. This place had more ramps than an eight lane highway—with jumps, bars and half pipes intricately designed throughout the unforgiving, cold concrete floor. As I perched myself comfortably to watch these athletes, I was surprised by my revelations. First, there seemed to be an unrehearsed synchronization amongst these fifty or sixty teenagers. Without a spoken word and not much more than the nod of their head, they systematically took their turns completely avoiding horrific collisions. It was like watching a well choreographed Broadway show. Second, they seemed to have a language all of their own, including words like 'grind', 'five-twenty', 'bowl' and 'tail grab'. Third and finally, this sacred building – this shrine – was no place for a tenderfoot as he would certainly stand out in this crowd of accomplished athletes.

Ron's debut was climactic, brief and completely hysterical. It premiered with Ron 'dropping' into what appeared to be a waterless, in-ground swimming pool. In only three seconds, he managed to completely obliterate my earlier revelations. This harmonized collection of gliding teenage athletes became rudely interrupted with a loud collision, followed by a chain reaction of numerous close calls. The secretive language was expanded upon with a few of Ron's unrepeatable, yet quite descriptive adjectives. And this private and exclusive teenager shrine was defiled – defiled by a neophyte.

As Ron spent the next twenty minutes attempting to aggressively crawl out of this ten foot deep, stair-less, soup bowl, his very proud son and all of his friends began to applaud his boldness and heroism. This cult-like group of incredible athletes had welcomed him into the fold. Ron glimpsed over and confidently waved thumbs up at me as he was embraced by his new flock of friends. Today, Ron endowed me with his wisdom! He had succeeded. Not at mastering the keen skills of boarding, but at mastering yet another enviable skill of parenting. Attaboy Ron! Something's very right I tell you! Something's very right!

I HOPE THESE KIDS START LOSING!

Something's very wrong I tell you! Something's very wrong! Why is it that as we move on in our years, it becomes less and less important to make new friends, and more important to hang onto those that we have. As a child, we make lasting friends by simply throwing the dodge ball towards the new kid. As a teenager, friends are vital to our existence and the more the better. As a twenty something year old, volume becomes less important and quality takes precedence. By the time we hit our late thirties and forties, our old friends are rock solid. And the desire and strength to build new friendships requires more caution, and remains a bit less desirable.

So here we are on the first practice session of the new season. As caring parents we spend all of our time prepping our kids about the months in front of them. We tell them about all the good things that we have heard about the new coach. We tell them that it's okay not to know anyone else on the team and that it's okay to be a little nervous about that. We tell them that many of the other kids feel the same way that they do. We tell them that making new friends will be very easy and we tell them that by the end of the first practice they will have brand new friends that they will enjoy for the rest of the season. And when we tell them all of these profound tidbits of wisdom, they believe us. And most importantly, we ourselves faithfully believe in the accuracy of this wisdom as we watch them leave the playing area with smiles and laughter glowing beneath their sweaty foreheads.

So if I profess it – and I believe it - and I witness the positive end result, then why do I completely fear that miserable first week of the new season when it becomes my turn to practice what I preach? Typically, like a heat sinking missile that finds its' warm target, I manage to always attract the one obsessed Dad who's in a hot pursuit of anyone who will listen to him. Lucky me!

Often, it's impossible to tell if he's 'one of them'. Early on he might resemble a normal Dad, engaging his victims in casual conversation – almost appearing likable. But then, typically before the third practice of the season, he begins to shed his disguise. As he emerges from his pod you begin to see evidence of his alien nature. His pleasant grin begins to fade to a tight lipped smirk. His ability to partake in non-sports conversation is replaced with sports trivia, boring statistics and mind numbing anecdotal stories of his child years in sports. He monopolizes the conversation from start to finish ensuring that we don't change the subject and move onto another conversation. He asks only a few questions in his tidal wave of speech – but clearly isn't interested in your response as he scrolls through his cell phone log or waves to other parents walking by briskly and without eye contact.

As the season progresses, it becomes quite apparent that I am this guy's only friend. Week after week, he begins his search and quickly finds me despite the creativity of my hiding spaces. If I am having discussions with other parents, he barges in, takes over the conversation until the group disperses. If I am sitting with relatives who have come to watch my son or daughter, he slides in, introduces himself and manages, in about one hour, to repeat every personal sports story I've been hearing throughout the entire season. Uggh! It's like fingernails on a blackboard.

Most sports seasons there is so much for us to look forward to. Some of our best and lasting friends were made at the Hockey rinks, Soccer fields and Basketball courts! And actually, I really enjoy meeting new people - new neighbors, new work colleagues, new church parishioners, or new members at my Gym. It's fun, educational and entertaining. But not this season. This season, I can only privately hope that our kids continue with their recent losing streak - not make the playoffs - and most importantly not extend this season - and my pain - for another month. Something's very wrong I tell you! Something's very wrong!

THE GENTLE
GIANT

Something's very wrong I tell you! Something's very wrong. I'm only ten years old, but I don't think that it's right that some big man called me fat. He was mean. He made me cry. I think I'm fat too. I know it already. But he still shouldn't have said it. He doesn't have good manners. I would like to tell him that he is not nice. I want to tell him that so badly. I want to yell at him as loud as I can when I tell him that. I think about that all the time. But I know that I won't ever do that. I won't do that because I have manners. I'm nice.

My best friend in the whole world is Anthony. He always played basketball. He was really good at it too. We played in his driveway almost every day after school. He taught me so much. We laughed all the time. We laughed so much sometimes our stomachs hurt. I didn't have a lot of friends in school. But that was okay, because I didn't need them. I had Anthony and that was just plenty. I love Anthony and I love basketball too.

One day Anthony told me about a fun league that was starting. It was a bunch of kids from a bunch of different schools. It was only for nine and ten year olds. Sometimes girls played too. That was cool. They played every Saturday morning at ten o'clock. There wasn't any practices during the week so my parents didn't have to worry about bringing me to places all over the world. I was so happy. My Dad said I could join as long as he didn't have to bring me every Saturday. That was okay because Anthony's Mom and Dad said they go every week and they watch the games and they could pick me up and then they could bring me home. I was so excited. Anthony was too. He said he would show me everything. He's played on lots of teams. He's wicked awesome at sports stuff. I've never been on a real team before. I never played a real sport. Just the sports on the video games but those aren't really, the real sports. But I'm pretty good at them, so I think I'll be pretty good at real basketball. My Dad doesn't think so. But he's never seen me play before. I know I'll get some points and I'm really tall too. My mom calls me the 'gentle giant' because I am taller and a lot heavier than other ten year olds. I think I will see girls there too because sometimes girls play too.

When we got there it was packed with tons and tons of people. They all came to watch the games that were being played. I'll have to tell my Dad that lots of other dads do come. It made me nervous to have that many people watching. I was very nervous. But I was very excited too. My stomach wasn't feeling good. Anthony's Mom told me it was just butterflies. I like her so much. She always treats me so nice. She says I'm like her second son and she's very proud of me and thinks that I am going to grow up and be very successful and famous. I think so too. We had to wait for the other games to finish before we could start. I waited in line with Anthony to get my first ever, real team tee shirt. We were blue. We were all going to wear blue shirts. We were going to look like a real basketball team you see on the television. The line was moving so slow. I couldn't wait to get my new shirt with my own number on it. I hope it's number 22. That's my favorite number.

But when I finally got to the front of the line they told me I couldn't have a shirt for the first few games. They had number 22 in the box but said they couldn't give me that one. They didn't tell me why. I think it was because I'm too fat. Maybe. I told them that I would take any number. I said please lots of times. But they said that I would have to wait, even though all the other kids got shirts. But I didn't care anymore. Well, for a little while I did care a lot, but not anymore. I just wanted to play basketball with Anthony on a real team. Our coach was awesome. He was Anthony's Dad's best friend. He liked me and called me his secret weapon. He said when he saw me warming up that I could catch the ball really good. I could catch it far above everyone else's head.

The game finally started. It took forever long to start. I didn't play right away but after a couple of buzzers went off I got into the game. I was pretty good too. I ran as hard as I could back and forth. Sometimes I didn't know the rules too good but the coach and the assistant coach and Anthony helped me. I caught the ball a lot. And sometimes when I did, I just ran with it to get closer to the net. I was supposed to dribble it, not run with it so much. I know that now. I'm not a good dribbler yet. It's pretty hard to do that and run at the same time. Some other kid on the other team kept stealing it from me. He was wicked good! The other team, the red team, was good. I heard someone say that they practiced together all the time even though they weren't supposed to. They were lucky.

There was a really pretty girl on the other team. I think her name was Heather. She went to my school. She said hi to me when she saw me in the tee shirt line. I felt a little silly not playing with a team shirt like everyone else, but I didn't care about that too much anymore. Just a little. Heather was awesome and she was a really good basketball player too. One time we were both on the court at the same time and I got to guard her. She was wicked fast and sometimes I couldn't keep up with her even though I tried. Her Dad was very loud when he was sitting in the bleachers.

He yelled at her all the time telling her what to do and how to do it. He didn't have many friends sitting around him like the other parents did. One time she caught the ball and dribbled it all the way down the other end of the court. She was so fast that I couldn't catch her. I really tried hard and ran as fast as I could go. I don't think I ever ran so fast in my entire life. But then all of a sudden Heather stopped really, really fast to take the shot. I didn't know that she was going to do that. I ran into her and knocked her over very badly. She was very small. She started crying and I felt very bad. I didn't mean to do that. I really didn't! I don't know why she stopped so quickly. I don't know if the ball went into the basket. I wasn't watching. I was only watching her cry. I said I was sorry really fast to her. I think that made her feel better. She wasn't crying so much after that.

The coaches from the other team came out to see if she was okay. Even our own coaches came to help her. I felt really bad. My coach winked at me and whispered that she was going to be fine. She had a bad scratch on her knees. I've had them too and they really hurt but they go away in about one week. Coach told me it was an accident and that it wasn't my fault. I think he was right because I didn't mean to do it. I like Heather a bunch. When I was walking off the floor back to the bench, Heather's Dad got very angry at me and began yelling so loudly that everyone in the entire place could hear him. He called me a fat _____. I'm not allowed to say the other words. He called me that three times. He said it so loudly that everyone on the planet and moon could hear him. When I got to the bench, I cried. But I cried so no one else could see me cry. Anthony sat next to me and helped to block the other kids from seeing me. I didn't want to play the rest of the game. Heather went home right away with her Dad so I couldn't tell her again that I was sorry. But I think she knew that I was really sorry.

I love basketball. I still play with Anthony but only in his driveway now. I wish I wasn't fat though.

Something's very wrong I tell you! Something's very wrong!

CAN HE SURVIVE IN SOCIETY?

Something's very wrong I tell you. Something's very wrong. Why do some adults absolutely insist on placing their child on a football field, basketball court or hockey rink – surround that child with all of his friends – invite family and neighbors to watch the game - then, proceed to humiliate, embarrass and chide that innocent child. Can someone please help me to understand this phenomenon? These misfit parents are apparently, reasonably intelligent people. They supposedly share some level of compassion for their children who provide them with unquestionable love. But put a uniform on these kids – a ball, a bat, a stick or a glove in their hands - call them a player - and that same parent morphs into the 'Critic from Hell'. All you have to do is watch any organized children's sport and very soon into the game play, the inevitable happens with the misfit parent, belting out insults and commands at his own flesh and blood.

All too many times I have wanted to just reach over, dope slap these misfit moms and dads and scream right back at them *"What are you doing to your child? What – are – you – doing?!"*. And then dope slap them a couple of more times just for the fun of it. But long before I can act, I get a reality check from my lovely bride as she gently squeezes my hand and lip syncs *"Let it go Tom. Let it go!"*. So, to help me deal with this reality situation, I need to drift off into a state of wonder and imagine how this doofus of a parent survives in the his adult society. Does he behave the same? Is he just as ignorant with other adults as he is with his own kids? I wonder! Does he publicly humiliate his boss? Does he flail insults at his mother in law?

Let's wonder together shall we? Imagine for a moment you are in the Annual meeting with your boss's boss, a room full of other folks, and this misfit parent happens to be your fellow coworker. The big boss is standing up at the front of the room emoting about the promising future of the company. He's spouting off statistic after statistic. He's cracking jokes that no one thinks are funny, but everyone still laughs at none the less. The boss is 'in the zone' – he's at the peak of his game – he's surrounded by a team who supports him. Sound familiar? Sound like your son on the football field right after he made a terrific first down catch, but couldn't get into the end zone for a touchdown? Enter the misfit Dad—who ejects himself into a gorilla like stance, emits some unintelligible grunting noise, pounds on the chairs in front of him and screams out loud *"What the hell are you doing Boss-man? Focus! Focus! Focus!"*.

Let's wonder again! Imagine for a moment, a beautiful, sunny, summer afternoon. Its July 4th weekend and the entire family are enjoying the outdoors and your wonderful backyard. The grandkids are in the pool, a few of the dads are flipping horseshoes and the ladies have just returned from a walk around the neighborhood. Trying her hardest to keep up with the rest of her younger, more capable, all-girl team is the elderly Great Aunt who you haven't seen in five years. She's walking quite a bit more slowly up the long, winding driveway. Sound familiar? Sound like your basketball daughter who just blocked 2 three-pointers in a row, but then couldn't leap that high for the third consecutive time? Enter the dumbbell Dad—who ignorantly blurts out *"Let's go Ole Lady! Let's go! Push it! Push it! Push it!"*.

Perhaps this is more appropriately a phenomenon about an adult who perpetually views his own child as someone less than a friend, someone less than a coworker or less than a distant relative, or perhaps even someone less than a stranger. While embarrassing one of these people in his life is probably not likely, it remains quite natural and convenient for him to embarrass his own loving child. So perhaps, this phenomenon isn't about an adult embarrassing his child after all. Perhaps it's more simply about an adult who continues to embarrass himself. Something's very wrong I tell you. Something's very wrong.

THE RABID
CREATURE

Something's very wrong I tell you. Something's very wrong! That's why I became trapped? Trapped, all alone with my eight year old son and his friends! My only thought was to protect him from the obsessed animal that was readying to attack. This rabid creature, flanked by a few of his mindless followers, had completely hypnotized and intimidated its innocent prey. They were ready to pounce - ready to come in for the kill. I was outnumbered. If I didn't act fast my son and his friends could be injured forever. I needed to defend them and defend them at any costs! I was about to take on this irrational beast and his cohorts. I was about to take on – the Hockey Dads!

The day began simple enough. A team of innocent children escorted by their unsuspecting parents to yet another weekend Hockey game. While we were suiting up before taking the ice, none of us noticed the creature lurking in the corner. Before the vicious attacks, some had reported the monster resembling the rest of us – acting like a normal Dad – some actually reported him smiling and laughing with his soon-to-be victims. Perhaps, after sensing the aroma of virgin blood, the creature began to transform to his natural being – like an abiding werewolf on the eve of a full moon.

So what was the catalyst that sparked the transformation of this mindless being? A simple question! A question that ignites the Jeckyl and Hyde. A question that alters the ordinary man into the maniacal Hulk monster. The question containing seven harmless words of—*"Did anyone see the game last night?"*. Apparently, during a televised, Hockey game the night before, one of the professional players, and I use the word professional quite loosely, was suspended for the next five games because he ignorantly and violently assailed another unsuspecting player, by sadistically flailing his rigid hockey stick toward an unsuspecting soft temple.

This seven-word question was like a lit cigarette being thrown into a vat of gasoline. Suddenly the brainless boogieman leaped to his feet, pounced to the middle of the floor, arched his back forward, dragged his knuckles gently on the cold concrete and ejected a hideous glare from his eyes. With the right corner of his lip pinched upwards, a drip of drool seeping out, and the complete captivation of the soon to be victims, he bellowed out with a deafening growl, *"What a game!"*

Surrounded by two of his adult allies, he then began his slow and painful assault on the minds of our precious children. For a brief moment though, his attack seemed harmless. Lecturing the room on *"What an idiot the player is!"* and how *"He should be fined big bucks"* and how *"He's jeopardizing the whole team by doin' somethin' like that!"*. Harmless? We could have only hoped. We quickly realized that this moment was fleeting at best and any hope of brilliance was immediately replaced with testosterone overload and stupidity. His attack continued with *"You never hit someone with a stick. Instead you throw your gloves down. You go to da guy when he ain't lookin'—and when he turns around you pound his face in with your bare fists. Now all you get is a ten minute penalty instead of five day suspension. This jerk shoulda known betta!!"*

We were shocked by the callous attack. While it was too late to save some of the children as evidenced by the glaze in their eyes and the affirmative nodding of their heads, I knew I could not give into this ignoramus. With a fire in my soul, I stood up to the enemy. I stared into my son's eight year old eyes, and begged of him and the other children—*"Don't listen to him! He doesn't know what he's talking about!"*. Then, something amazing happened. My little boy responded, with utmost sincerity, *"I know Dad."*. My strength renewed, I intently stared slowly across the room, receiving acknowledgement from so many that I had saved, until finally focusing on the enemy. He heard my growl. He heard my son's growl. The animal retreated. No defense. No offense. He simply retreated into the corner - appearing almost tamed. Something's very wrong I tell you. Something's very wrong.

My Foxhole
Buddy

Something's very wrong I tell you! Something's very wrong! Some people simply cannot fathom the concept of teamwork! So what's the first sport that comes to mind when you think about teamwork? A. Football? B. Yachting? C. Synchronized Swimming? D. None of the Above. If you chose D, you are correct-oh-mun-doh! The only sport that requires life saving, pain free teamwork—Paintball!

Think about it! When a teammate screws up – you die – and so do all of your colleagues who don those insect looking, bug-eyed face masks. Well OK, they don't really die – but if you have ever been shot square in the chest with one of those marble-sized, paint filled, hard shelled projectiles, traveling at speeds of up to three hundred miles per hour, you would swear for just a brief moment that your lungs completely forgot how to exhale and were stuck in a permanent state of inhale.

So, for the benefit of all you yellow belly cowards, who have never engaged yourself in this sport, allow me to provide this brief introduction. Most of the time these games are played in large, football sized fields that are filled with numerous bunkers that you can easily hide behind - I mean strategically place yourself behind. Teams come in all different sizes and they chose from a variety of games that last anywhere between five and twenty minutes. But perhaps the most popular game is the age-old 'Capture the Flag'. The objective of this game hasn't changed in decades. Simply capture the other teams' flag and return it to your home base without being shot. Each player carries a Paintball Marker (commonly referred to by the Novice as a "gun") loaded with up to two hundred paintballs. The only other required piece of equipment – a face mask – an essential tool needed to prevent permanent blindness.

As barbaric as this growing sport may sound to those over-opinionated, 'no one asked you' onlookers, it is truly a game of strategy, teamwork and more importantly, honor. Like the game of golf, it provides numerous opportunities to cheat and take unfair advantages. It's also a sport that embraces all of its players in an addictive, adrenaline rush that is hard to find in most legal activities. Your success depends on a dual strategy. Under no circumstance do you want to get tagged with one of those miserable, brightly colored, painfully stinging paintballs. But at the same time you must be completely focused on instilling that pain directly into the human beings on the other side of that playing field. Ahhhh, what a rush!

Well, as you can imagine, the need to work closely with your team is essential. The last thing any team needs is that crazy rebel who's 'gonna do it on his own'. I however, am apparently cursed with the unique ability to attract these jackass fathers like a giant trout attracts every wannabe fisherman in a fifty mile radius. On this beautiful, Fall Sunday afternoon, I find myself quite anxious to begin this long awaited Father vs. Son paintball tournament. The Sons were spanning in age from twelve to seventeen and the Fathers were spanning in rage from *"Let's have some fun!"* to *"Let's kick their bony little butts!"*.

As this team of balding, beer-bellied Pops began to plan their strategy, this James Dean rebel Dad, could have honestly cared less about anything that resembled teamwork and unity. Shooting balls into the sky—lifting his mask because it blocked his vision—taunting the boys three hundred feet away *"You're dead meat, you're dead meat"*—and bragging about the numerous black and blues, welts and sores he had from his last time playing. Oh god, what an idiot he was!

So, as only my life will have it, I draw the short straw and get partnered with this fool from Idiotville. As I sprint for the first bunker, huffing and puffing, wondering if my wonderful son is as excited as I am, I get shoved from behind by 'Johnny do-it-alone' looking to share the smallest bunker on the entire field. As he does a Rambo-like slide, face first into the dirt, he grunts quite sophomorically *"Hey Dude!"*. That's right. He called me Dude. Needless to say, Daddy dumbbell gave up our location, compromised the entire teams' well orchestrated mission, and left his foxhole buddy, me, to get lambasted with more paint splatter than a Sherwin Williams drop cloth. Something's very wrong I tell you. Something's very wrong.

I'LL NEVER EAT FRIED CHICKEN AGAIN

Something's very wrong I tell you. Something's very wrong! Why would a perfect stranger think that I am the least bit interested in the dreadfully boring athletic history of his seven year old daughter? For gosh sakes, she's seven years old!! Is it possible that any seven year old could have nearly enough lifetime experiences to completely dominate a painfully long, two hour conversation? NO! Absolutely not! But this dumbbell Dad somehow managed to successfully stretch out her insignificant and meaningless accomplishments to read like an unabridged version of War and Peace. I never found out how this Dad earned a living but I would confidently guess that it has something to do with mountains and mole hills.

So there I was, at a wonderful house party at my best friends, celebrating his son's graduation from college. After many pleasant hellos, congratulatory wishes and *"long time no see"* conversations, I had eventually wiggled my way through the crowd to my most favorite place on earth – the buffet table. I floated my way through this incredible paradise of picnic carbohydrates, carefully palming my extra strength, plastic plate to sustain the pressures of my food pyramid. My nirvana was interrupted with a deep, vibrating, voice of *"Mmm, mmm, that fried chicken sure looks good, huh?!"*. Obviously, this stranger appeared to be a brilliant man who shared my appreciation for the finer things in life. Little did I know – and was soon to find out – that this fried chicken worship was no more than a secret, cult code amongst dumbbell dads. It was nothing but a ruse to kidnap incredibly smart and overwhelmingly handsome dads—to kidnap me while I was at my most vulnerable, human state—the state of hunger.

On this unexpected, rainy day, I found one lonely, remaining seat in this massively, overcrowded home. It was here that I could safely rest my salad plate, dessert plate and drink. It was here that I could allow my main course plate to perform a private lap dance on the thighs of my legs. Ahhh, my little piece of heaven! Just as I was to indulge in this angelic feast, I looked up from my comfortable corner chair to find the cult leader smiling down on me. He was licking the last remnant of potato salad from the fork prongs, while exposing a mouth jam-packed with the same. After a brief sharing of first names, he was quick to point out his daughter standing on the other side of the room. She was adorable. I later found out that she was the youngest of three with two older brothers, who I'm guessing did not participate in organized sports, as the dumbbell Dad struggled to even, mention their names.

With absolutely no interest in who I was, or how I knew the graduating student—he literally began the slow, painful history at the birth of his daughter. He knew at that very moment that she was going to be an incredible athlete due to the spans of her legs and the width of her biceps. (Normal dads would refer to this as adorable, baby fat! But I digress) As he arduously tortured me through each painful year of her life, I actually began to find my level of interest transforming. Let me be clear. It was far from an interesting story and was actually borderline suicidal, but I discovered myself mysteriously hypnotized by his obviously well rehearsed script. It was sort of like that 2AM movie you started watching on channel 819 because you couldn't sleep. While it completely sucked, you actually forced yourself to stay awake because you just had to see how it was going to end – only to be incredibly disappointed.

If his meticulously detailed, list of boring events wasn't enough, it became painfully worse when he related each of her accomplishments to his gene pool and his own high school and college experiences. As I think back to that miserable storyteller, I often wonder if he would have been equally as excited if she decided to be an accomplished violinist or the second grade spelling bee champion. I often wonder how the two non-athletic brothers deal with the obvious lack of attention. I often wonder how he describes his wife.

Not once in this two hour ordeal, did he ask me if I had children or if I was married or if I was interested in sports. Not one complete sentence exited this dumbbell's lips that didn't reference sports, his background or his daughter's future as a high paid, professional athlete. Not once did he read my body language as a complete lack of interest. Not once did he interrupt his wordy momentum even as other partygoers tried to step into the conversation and perhaps rescue me. The only breather he managed to take was to suck another chicken bone clean while grunting out yet another *"Mmmm, awesome!"*. I haven't been able to eat fried chicken since. Something's very wrong I tell you! Something's very wrong!

KISSING YOUR BELLY BUTTON

Something's very wrong I tell you, something's very wrong. How does a parent not get emotionally overwhelmed and obsessed when his child is at bat, in the bottom of the ninth inning, down by one run with one man on base. I would have thought that was a physical incapability –like kissing your own belly button.

But? There was Dad! His head was buried into his laptop computer with little clue as to what was happening around him. The families on both sides were jumping and screaming like fighting ally cats. The players in one of the dugouts were chanting a church-like rhythm of *"Let's—Go—Batter!"*, while the opposing dugout was harmonizing to a congo-beat of *"No batter – No batter – No batter!"*. And the best we got from the misfit laptop loving Dad? A swatting of a mosquito, an adjustment to his eyeglasses and a glance at his wristwatch.

So who is this Clark Kent look alike? He's no Superman, that's for sure! You remember him though. He's an amalgamation of all the weird kids you went to High School with. The nerd - the loner - the kid who never showered after gym class – the kid who stared at you until you looked back – the kid who sarcastically giggled when someone gave the wrong answer! This walking-human-anomaly certainly hasn't changed much over the years.

So you've got to wonder what this schmuck is doing as he's laughing awkwardly at his laptop and remains completely oblivious to his child's crowning moment. Could it be his job? Maybe. Could he be playing the new *"I'm an Idiot"* video game? That's my bet!. Could he be surfing the web for 'Father of the Year Awards?' No chance! No chance at all!

Suddenly, on this terrific, warm and sunny day, half of the raucous crowd went absolutely wild with joy, excitement and enthusiasm!! There was screaming that could only be identified as deafening and spine tingling! While some boys leaped and ricocheted from an adrenaline high, others sadly and slowly dragged themselves off of the playing field. Parents on both sides offered sincere congratulations while others offered pats on the back and words of encouragement. And what would Superman do as his Kryptonite-like child approached him? How would he explain missing his son's incredible base hit that drove in the winning run of the game? He wouldn't have to. His son struck out! Something's very wrong I tell you. Something's very wrong!

My Daughter
the Addict

Something's very wrong I tell you! Something's very wrong! I stand alone as an innocent victim of an elaborate conspiracy. A well orchestrated, intellectual scheme that blindsided me like a 2x4 across my backside! It was an obnoxious plot ranging from blood sucking multi-million dollar corporations; to struggling, small business owners; to my very own, my sweet, and my precious sixteen year old daughter. How did this boardroom full of suit and tie strangers brainwash my innocent bundle of joy and convince her to reach into my pocket and pick me clean – like a young, impassioned, con artist working his elderly prey.

My daughter was an addict. From her first high, she was desperately hooked. There was no turning back. She needed it again and again. So here we were, another Saturday night – only minutes before her next injection. My sweet angel focused only on her imminent fix. Her adrenaline flowing. Her nerves shot. Her muscles tight and her heart pumping like a sump in a flood zone. Suddenly, yet precisely on schedule, she's blinded by a bright light and deafened by a thunderous roar of raw skin slapping against raw skin. Finally, it was here - opening night of her dance recital. My daughter's natural high has begun.

The scam began on a cool spring night. My daughter arrived home with a smile on her face that reached from one dangling earring to the next. As happy as she could be, she bellowed out, *"Hi Daddy! How's it going?"* And there were my first three clues that I was in deep financial trouble. Clue # 1: *"Hi"* – the fact that my teenage daughter actually demonstrated an interest in being within a seven mile radius of either parent. Clue # 2: *"Daddy"* – an actual term of endearment. It wasn't *"Pops"*, it wasn't *"Yo!"*

It wasn't *"Hey, where's Mom?"* Clue # 3: *"How's it going?"* My teenager demonstrating an interest in someone else's life other than her own? I was now quite certain that her next sentences were going to inflict a significant dent into my already '3-kid-thin' wallet.

"Daddy, I have such incredible news! You're not going to believe it! My dance team was selected to perform live, 3 different nights, on a cruise ship to some exotic island. Do you believe it? What an honor! What an honor! Our dance instructor surprised us tonight with the news! Isn't that unbelievable?! I can't believe it. I'm so excited! I'll need to buy all new clothes – get my nails done – get my hair done – cha ching, cha ching, cha ching." Well, after a series of questions, and a couple of phone calls to other parents, it appears as though my princess' story was accurate, down to the finest detail. We were so excited for her. An all expense paid Caribbean cruise, hanging with her friends all week, a few chaperones to keep them all in check. Wow! What an experience for a kid!

At the next rehearsal, the axe fell quickly as all the hands began quickly reaching into my wallet and bank account. Apparently, this – selection process – and this - high honor we heard about only a few nights earlier – had absolutely nothing at all to do with selection and honor. The gimmick requires the dance troupe to perform for one hour a night for three nights as part of the cruise ship entertainment. Other than that, there's no further commitment from the kids. Oh yah – there's a catch (Gee! There's a surprise huh?) Each of the thirty children in the troupe need to have one parent chaperone them on the cruise. Oh yah – just one more catch. Each dancer AND their parental chaperones pay the full fare for the cruise.

The cruise line sells sixty full rate fares during an off season while only giving away four free trips to the dance studio owner. The cruise line gets free entertainment. The studio owner gets the 'all expense' paid vacation of a lifetime. My daughter remains in her euphoric high. And my lovely wife helped me to understand that it should be her, not I, to accompany our daughter on this Caribbean experience, because of female, mother, daughter, blah, blah, blah. Something's very wrong I tell you. Something's very wrong.

GRAMPY THE CAVEMAN

Something's very wrong I tell you! Something's very wrong! No, not with the idiotic Dad who pushes his son beyond all physical and emotional limits while he lives his life vicariously through the eyes of his son. No. Not the moronic Mom who stands on the sidelines screeching meaningless cheers to the children, for the sole purpose of annoying the parents on the opposing team. But instead, someone please tell me what is up with a Grandfather who tells his nine year old grandson to stop talking about *"becoming a professional athlete one day, because it's a waste of time"*. Hello! Earth to pinhead! Earth to numskull! Now I've occasionally heard that fools like this still existed. But I thought they were only stories, fiction, unicorns, and legends. I never believed that an actual caveman could be walking the planet today!

As my nine year old son and I were waiting in an incredibly long line to register for the local town hockey tournament, there was a subdued and somewhat anxious couple in front of us. Standing quietly was an elderly grey haired, lanky gentleman, whose frame was slightly bent and twisted. His large hand was being held quite firmly by five tiny fingers that were attached to the body of an extremely antsy and aspiring hockey player. The bug eyed, bright smiling little boy, bouncing on the balls of his feet, looked up at his father's father and professed with a huge air of confidence, *"Grampy? When I grow up I'm going to be a professional hockey player!"* What kid hasn't had this type of dream? To be a famous athlete, a super hero, a cartoon character, or a ninja warrior?! Then, with a biting, irritable response, Grampy the moron barks back, with a jolt of the youngsters arm, *"Don't be silly! You can't be a real hockey player. Who's filling your head with that junk anyway?"* Even my own son turned to me, replacing the earlier smile on his face with a question mark expression that spanned ear to ear.

At first my emotions were uncontrollably drawn toward that poor little boy. He was just advised by someone he undoubtedly loves, to not do your best, to stop wishing, to stop trying, to stop dreaming! Like the special effects in a movie, I watched the vibrant energy slowly and effortlessly drain from this boy's little body. It physically hurt my heart to watch him turn so limp. Embarrassed, he nervously looked around to see what other school mates and friends might have overheard his Grampy's assessment. Then, faster than an NHL slapshot, my emotions whipsawed to anger and frustration. As I watched Grampy the villain stand there, glaring at his watch, remaining utterly clueless to his repugnant execution of his grandson's spirit and wonderment, I found myself completely unable to control my next actions.

So instead of simply minding my own business and keeping this incredibly large mouth of mine firmly shut, I turned to the little boy and said, *"Honey, I'll bet you Grampy thinks you shouldn't be a hockey player because he thinks you'll be a much better football or baseball player, or maybe a fireman who saves lives, or who knows – maybe the next President of the United States."* As I saw the double dimples return to his smile and the glimmer of hope return to his personality, I now focused my attention to Grampy, the King of Buffoons. As he turned his crooked body toward me, with his lower jaw falling and beginning to form a word, I did to him what I have only seen both my wife and mother successfully do. I gave him— THE LOOK! I simply had no idea that I possessed this incredible power. I not only possessed it but I was a master of its flawless delivery. As I have been victimized by this death stare several times in my own life by very powerful women, I knew instantly of its overwhelming effects. With just one, immediate, piercing glance, I disemboweled this elderly fool. With only the daggers that emitted from my hazel eyes and without saying one word, I forced him to not only rethink the last three minutes of his life, but the last fifty or so years of his child rearing experiences.

I often wonder how Grampy has survived such a long life consumed with low expectations, little hope and lesser effort. I wonder if he's ever told his Doctor to stop trying so hard. I wonder if he's ever told his auto mechanic to stop being silly and not fix the braking system on his car. Most importantly, I wonder if the grandson will ever figure out that his Grampy is just a useless dork, or will love overpower common sense and cause the grandson to simply stop dreaming – stop trying? Something's very wrong I tell you! Something's very wrong!

INSANITY VANITY PLATES

Something's very wrong I tell you! Something's very wrong! Have you ever seen the vanity license plates with the obscure little messages that only mean something to the person that's driving the vehicle? They should be outlawed! They're dangerous! It never fails – I'm usually the guy who's behind the sports car late at night, on a winding road in pouring rain. With the plate in front of me just barely visible, I struggle to make out some stupid, nebulous message printed on the fluorescent background: *S-C-E-N-T-S*. What the hell does that mean? SCENTS? What's scented? The paint job – apple red? The driver – wreaking of alcohol? What is it that the owner wants me to think when I see that message? Is she telling me she just purchased it and it has that new car scent? Is it an acronym for South Carolina Environmental blah blah blah something or other? What's the true meaning hiding behind this entire metal, glow in the dark world of advertisements?

Vanity plates? They should call them Insanity plates. Each one I see makes me crazier than the one before. Most of them not only drive me crazy, they practically drive me off the road as I obsess with their meanings. But I can forget about all of that now! It's Friday night and that means high school football. And as we arrive at the field to watch our neighbor's teenage son play in an age old town to town rivalry, guess what pounces out at me as we search for a precious parking spot. Surrounding me, like jackals on a bloody carcass – those insanity vanity plates - everywhere I look. *XTRAPNT* and *WELUVNFL* and *PIGSKINS*. Aarrgghhh!!!! They're everywhere!!!

And then it hit me like the smell of week old fish in a metal trash bin on a hot summer day!! A great idea! It's an idea that will make me rich beyond my wildest dreams. I'm going to sell custom vanity plates to the parents of high school kids enrolled in athletics, student council and community theatre. Now for the fist time, parents will be able to advertise their child's accomplishments and boast to the whole world, what they have known all along.

For the mom who knew at the moment of birth, when her baby daughter was still covered in blood and amniotic fluids, that she would be a world famous movie star – we offer – *CMYMOVIE?*.

For the dad who lives vicariously through the eyes of his freshman Basketball player – we offer – *MJORDAN2*.

For the retired soccer mom who loaded her van with half of the team and drove them to every game and every practice in a one hundred fifty mile radius – we offer – *NOMOTAXI*.

For the parents who spent hundreds of dollars for professionally designed posters, pins and banners for their daughter's student council elections – we offer – *NEXTPRES*.

For the dad who dreams about sitting in the gallery of the eighteenth hole as his son walks up to the green amidst deafening applause– we offer – *TIGERWHO?*

And for that ever growing population of extreme parents, we offer these generic insanity plates that are sure to bring continuous smiles to their faces. *GOINPRO* and *IMTHEBEST* and *ALLBOUTME* and *JUSTME* and my personal favorite, *OTHRSSUCK*.

And of course we would have additional products for sale such as oversized, glow in the dark, bumper stickers. Clearly the most popular sticker purchased in every state in the nation would be *"THIS TEAM IS NOTHING WITHOUT MY SON"*.

Millions! I'll be worth millions! The market for these products continues to grow at an accelerating rate. I will be able to ask any price I want and these euphoric, over aggressive parents will throw bundles of cash at my feet. I'm even going to have my very own special insanity plate made. Painted with real gold leaf on a solid platinum background, it will read: *ITSWRONG*. Something's very wrong I tell you! Something's very wrong.

THE M.I.A. MOM.

Something's very wrong I tell you! Something's very wrong! Would you ever give your nine year old child a loaded gun to play with? How about a set of sharpened knives to juggle? How about putting her in a Kayak and sending her down the white water, level five rapids of the Colorado River? Then why, why, why would you attach a couple of pieces of fiberglass sticks to his feet – abandon him on top of a magnificent mountain buried in snow and ice and encourage him to push off—ALL ALONE?

I actually asked those questions and a few additional ones to a Mom of a nine year old. And to no surprise, all of the ditzy Mom's responses supported her complete absence of common sense - and endorsed her selfish, all-about-me personality. Of course, I guess it's entirely possible that my blunt portrayal of her could be inaccurate - as I could not completely understand some of her responses when she talked directly into her Hot Toddy cup that was being refilled yet once again, by the very busy and apparently very annoyed bartender.

But, back to the nine year old - a nine year old who I *(and several other responsible adults)* involuntarily adopted for most of that sunshine filled day while on that spectacular New Hampshire Mountain. My first introduction to Jason came as I swooshed by him while in hot pursuit of catching up with my three children; who were waiting - quite impatiently I might add - at the predetermined 'stop spot'. In obvious pain, Jason had positioned himself off to the far side of the trail, bending over in nearly a ninety degree angle, burying his hands under his coat and into his lower stomach. He needed help and I was there! Like a superhero I swooshed over to his aid! I came to an immediate stop – well an eventual one anyway – once I stopped sliding that is. After several attempts, I was able to finally stand back up with only minor damage to my self esteem. My kids were laughing quite heartily at their old man's face-plant. But I was able to quickly get even as I signaled them to walk back up the mountain fifty or so yards to assist with Jason. Oh yah, I was a real popular Dad that day.

As I quickly befriended Jason, he informed me that he dropped one of his ski gloves while he was on the chair lift. He had skied for more than an hour after that and his soft, little hand had become glowing red and completely numb to the touch. I asked if he was with anyone else and he quite independently retorted, *"No, my Mom doesn't ski".* Later conversations with my new found buddy Jason revealed that Mommy Dearest typically drops him off at the base of the mountain, and then proceeds to browse in the dozens of boutique shops that line the slopes. And when she can no longer handle the pressures of her strenuous and high pressure day, she stops in one of the several bars to rest and relax. I had loaned Jason my warm glove and encouraged him to *"hang with the family"* until we could locate his MIA Mom (Mother Is an Ass). Jason was just a great kid, who was pretty excited about the unexpected attention, and even more excited about the opportunity to show off his skiing talents to someone with interest.

Eventually, we caught up with Bambi. I'm not sure if that's her real name but it 'just sounds right'. Actually, she seemed quite happy to see Jason. Of course, at that point in her early day, she was quite happy with just about everything and everyone. I introduced myself and explained that we found him more than three hours ago in the middle of a black diamond trail. I also let it be known that several other folks and resort employees participated in the search for Bambi and that several calls to her cell phone went unheeded. I told her she didn't need to worry about getting Jason lunch as I took care of that a while ago. Jason showed her the new pair of gloves I bought him in the local boutique (which required long term financing options). I also gave her the good news that the Ski Patrol did not think that Jason's hand was frostbit – but was probably very close to it.

Obviously, I failed miserably in penetrating her thick skull with my emotion and logic. Her incredibly selfish response included something resembling an ugly, full body spasm – followed by an embarrassing, high pitched squeal - directed at her child blaming him for *"ruining her day"*. And as sweet little Jason had obviously done thousands of times before – he raised his whimpering eyes and softly spoke *"I'm sorry Mommy!"*. There's no doubt that this day was complete with losses. My kid's lost several hours of great skiing conditions. I lost a few bucks on clothing and feeding a stranger. Jason lost his mitten and Mommy lost what little dignity she still had. With a mom like Bambi, it is painfully obvious that this is not the first, nor the last mountain, that poor little Jason will have to climb alone. Something's very wrong I tell you! Something's very wrong!

THOSE ANGELIC VOLUNTEERS

Something's very wrong I tell you! Something's very wrong! Why can't I be a volunteer coach on one of these kid's sports teams? I'm a good guy. I like sports. I'm great with kids. Kids love my sense of humor. They respond well to me. I know how to teach and what it takes for kids to learn. And best of all, as my lovely wife reminds me quite regularly, I all too often act like a kid myself. So why can't I coach then? A simple reason—psycho parents! One thing is for certain. My first week on the job I'd end up in jail for popping some clueless father smack dab in the nose, or calling some dreadful mother a long list of unrepeatable names.

There is no doubt that God has a special place in Heaven for all of these wonderful, volunteer coaches. And the praise and respect goes well beyond the coaching staff all the way to the team managers, the schedulers, and the entire cast behind the scenes that ensure all of our kid athletes have a season filled with enjoyment, laughter, lessons and memories. They not only coordinate the weekly games and practices, but the fundraisers, season ending cookouts and award celebrations as well. Through all the years that my kids have been engaged in organized sports, I have never met a coach I didn't like (Well. Actually, there was just one. Keep reading.) and I've met only an occasional few that I have had different opinions from, but never one, never one that I disliked. Psycho parents on the other hand? Well, I have a list of stories long enough to write several best selling books!

And while most of the team parents truly appreciate these angel volunteers, there is that persistent, annoying, blackboard scratching, minority of ignoramuses that consistently manage to openly criticize the coaches while privately consuming more of the coaches time than the kid's themselves. The well renowned business management guru, Doctor Joseph Juran must have had his children enrolled in local sports programs when he coined his 80/20 principle as "20 percent of the defects cause 80% of the problems". Defect! A completely accurate term - and I love it!

Week after week, these Defect-parents begin their ritual like a smoldering hot ash hidden under a bed of dry autumn leaves. The minute the Defect arrives at the game he's blowing off smoke about the last game, or the line up, or how the coach screwed up the season. His voice starts low, only being heard by those within an ear shot. Half way through the game the smoke turns into first flame as he relocates himself to the top of the bleachers. And as the game reaches its close, he's evolved into a towering inferno belching one derogatory comment after another at the entire coaching staff. *"Hey coach, did you come to watch or coach?"* – or – *"C'mon coach. Do something! Anything!"* – or – *"Yoah coach? You do know that there are two teams out there, right?"*

While most of the parents would like to put out this Defects fire by sucking the oxygen directly from his lungs, he somehow, always manages to recruit one dimwit ally who joins by his side and fuels the flame instead. And the two of them, like an intense game of ping pong, exchange barb after barb of unjustified, abusive insults. So self absorbed are they that they completely forget there are other parents, grandparents and children all around them. And just when you thought it was over, one last burst of flames explode from the two gasbags with *"Oh no! Coach? What the hell are you doing you (expletive) idiot?"*

Then? Silence! So much silence one could hear those autumn leaves falling thunderously to the ground. As we all glare at the Defects, we see a very familiar and outwardly distraught Mom and her tear filled children abruptly leave their seats. The coach's wife and the coach's children had heard enough! Something's very wrong I tell you! Something's very wrong!

Super-Kids? No Thanks!

Something's very wrong I tell you! Something's very wrong! Whatever happened to teaching a child important lessons that will prove invaluable in his adulthood? Whatever happened to teaching a child the skills and talents necessary to thrive in a diverse and demanding society? Instead, I all too often encounter mothers and fathers who have lost all focus on these human life lessons. They genuinely see their child as some type of super hero – some 'super-kid' athlete that teams, coaches and players would be overwhelmed and honored to play with. They are solidly convinced that their son or daughter should be catered to and pampered over. They religiously believe that the formal and casual rules of any sport are not for their children, but for all the peasant children. Of course, these hypnotized parents seem to be the only living creatures that hold their super-kid in such high regard. On the contrary, the hallways and locker rooms are filled with clandestine and emotional conversation from other adults and kids about the disruptive, selfish and overpowering nature of the 'super-kid'.

Our coaches and parents had decided months earlier to enter the team into a regional tournament. Our arch rivals throughout the regular season were also competing in this weekend long competition. Our first game would be Friday night, against them. We knew we were bigger, faster and stronger this year and stood a good chance of beating them and even possibly winning the entire tournament. Both kids and adults were looking forward to what is typically a fun and energized sports rivalry.

Commitments from the families had to be provided well in advance. Deposits needed to be mailed and hotel rooms had to be reserved while there were still vacancies. We understood that we would not be able to field a full team as some families had unavoidable conflicts with their schedules. We knew in advance that we would be a lean and mean team with very few substitutes. The kids would truly have to depend on each other and crank it up a notch or two. They would have to work hard. They would be exhausted after every game. But, if they stuck together, they would actually have a great chance of going all the way.

It was a typical brownish-orange, cold fall day in New England. Thirty minutes before the start of the game the coach announced some significant changes to player positions and starting lineups. He did a terrific job explaining the what's and why's of the changes. The kids had heard the same speech just minutes earlier and none of them had an issue. As a matter of fact, many of them were looking forward to the challenge and trying something new. All of the parents had embraced the exciting changes too. Well, almost all the parents anyway. Enter, Mr. and Mrs. Imbecile! They masqueraded as parents by day and wannabe Sports Agents by night. They were simply infuriated that their godlike, holier than thou son, would not be playing his traditional position, and would instead be relegated to an inferior position typically reserved for the lesser, human-like children.

For the rest of this critical game, Mr. & Mrs. Imbecile, who go by their first names of HesA and ShesA, made it a point for all of us to hear their persistent moaning and griping. Like overweight cows grazing for a greener pasture, they moved from one parent to the next looking for someone who would listen; someone who could feed their anger. Despite our crushing victory over these long time rivals, the utter joy of our kids, and the opportunity to move onto the next round of competition, the entire Imbecile family was no where to be found the next morning. They had simply disappeared, leaving the team of exhausted, yet exhilarated young men to fend for themselves. Like a spoiled young child who takes his new ball and stomps his feet, the parents from Fantasy Land took their son and went home. By the following week, they had officially quit the team and left the town league all together. And guess who the son showed up playing for a short time later? Our arch rivals!

Now let's fast forward in time. It's the first practice of our new season and guess who returns, walking brazenly into the playing area? The Messiah – followed confidently and boldly by the same two ignoramus parents who yanked him from the team and league just two years earlier. We soon learned that after he abandoned us with complete disregard to join the enemy, he later dumped them, joined another team, only to walk out on them as well, and ultimately return to bless us with his godlike presence once again. Lucky us, huh?

Don't get me wrong. This kids a good little athlete, but he's far from a prodigy. Perhaps he stands a bit of a better chance than most, of making his high school team. But that's it. Period. I don't blame him for his arrogance and pomposity. He's just a kid who learns that behavior from HesA and ShesA. They're the ones that irritate me more than boxer shorts lined with poison oak. I don't know a lot about them. I'm not about to learn much more either since it's not likely that I will ever be able to muster up enough patience or self restraint to have more than a fifteen second conversation with them. But what types of parents teach their kids a lack of responsibility to oneself? When you start something – you finish it! What types of parents teach their kids a lack of commitment to authority? You made a commitment to the coach — you honor it! What types of parents teach their kids a lack of dependability to others? The team needs you — no matter what!

As this boy grows, he will undoubtedly reach adulthood by chronological and legal standards. But, he'll truly never reach adulthood by maturity standards. His parents set him up to fail in this regard. He is certain to spend his life absent of all blame and finding fault with everyone around him. His divorce will be his wife's fault. His unhappiness will be his kid's fault. His unemployment will be his last bosses fault. His house foreclosure will be the government's fault. Something's very wrong I tell you! Something's very wrong!

Johnny, the Angel of Death

Something's very wrong I tell you! Something's very wrong! Why is it that some people think the rules that govern our society don't apply to them? Why is it that these same people are the first people to complain when someone else violates those very same rules. I'm not talking about written laws. I'm not talking about the two hundred and fifty dollar fine for parking in a handicapped zone. As far as I'm concerned, any selfish, moronic and uncaring scum who does that should be tied up behind fifty motorized wheel chairs and dragged through the town square. I'm not talking about the alcoholic-in-denial who still chooses in this day and age to put his inebriated ass behind a steering wheel and jeopardize the safety of all of our families. He not only deserves time in jail, he deserves time trapped and squeezed between two panes of glass that serve as the front window of a liquor store. What I am talking about is the unwritten rules – aka manners – aka common sense. Things like talking on your cell phones while in a movie theatre. Things like a simple apology for bumping shoulders in a crowded hallway. Things like assuming that because I am a volunteer coach that somehow automatically enrolls me into the job of being your child's babysitter.

So here I was, suddenly thrown into the middle of fifteen energetic, perpetually laughing, six year old boys and girls. They were actually expecting me to teach them the fundamentals of this wonderful sport of Soccer. Little did they and their parents know that I took a crash course studying the rules of soccer, just the night before. As I have said in the past, I would love to coach kids. But I know my limits and I would undoubtedly be arrested sooner or later for punching some moronic dad in the nose or cussing out some imbecile mom. And until some law is passed that permanently bans doofus parents from all organized sports, then coaching was not a line item that would ever appear on my resume. But this was a special situation. By the second week of the new season, both the assistant coach and the head coach had to leave for personal and professional reasons. My decision to help out the league and the kids was exclusively driven by the desperate plea of a bright eyed, hereditarily handsome, six year old boy who said, *"Oh Dad, it would be so wicked cool, really neat if you could coach my team. C'mon dad! Please? Please? Please?"*

It was a miserably hot, hazy and humid summer day. I patiently awaited the arrival of my new recruits. I was well adorned I might add, in my new spandex Soccer shirt, my new Soccer shorts and my pristine clean, shiny athletic sneakers. Despite the oppressive climate, my band of six year old athletes arrived quite anxious to start their practice session. They all came prepared with an ice cold water bottle attached to their tiny hands, and a backup bottle resting vertically in the cooler, situated neatly by the feet of their anxious, spectator parents. And like a piece of sticky candy on a hot sidewalk attracts ants, I undoubtedly attracted a human size insect of my very own. Her name was Sue – the annoyed mother of Johnny. Six year old Johnny walked alone, onto the field, at least one hundred yards from the closest parking lot. I'm assuming 'simple Sue' dropped him off in the parking lot, but I certainly wouldn't be surprised if she made him stand on the side of the road with his thumb out.

Johnny was just the type of kid you would expect him to be. He was a terror! A four foot high tower of absolute, miserable terror. The only adult this kid ever respected was the chain-smoking clerk at the video store who regularly fed Johnny's obvious, junkie-like habit of video game addictions. Within his first three minutes on the field, he had punched and pushed one boy, scratched another girl across the neck, and drop kicked the only soccer ball they gave me into the murky, stagnant swamp water - which by the way, was very carefully concealed below the tall grass I ran through to fetch the ball. As I reluctantly returned to the playing field in my soaking wet, mud filled athletic sneakers; I tried to find out who the unfortunate parent was of this child criminal. No one stood up from their chair to claim him. No one raised a hand in acknowledgement. Then it hit me. Oh my God!! The child from hell was my responsibility. I was his babysitter!

Where was Mom? How could she have done this to me? She's never met me. She didn't even know if I was on the field when she dropped him off. How does she know I didn't cancel or move the practice last minute? How does she know her precious little angel (of death!) isn't aimlessly walking the streets of New Hampshire? I've never met simple minded Sue but I know already that I don't like her very much. As I was daydreaming about the fifty top things I would like to say to simple Sue, I was rudely interrupted with *"Hey Mister? I'm thirsty!"*. So before Johnny decided to rob or brutalize one of his teammates for water, I quickly handed over my unopened bottle to him.

The rest of the practice continued with all of the other angelic children listening, having fun, participating, and trying hard. Johnny just continued to do his own thing; including parking his butt in one of the other parents' chairs and refusing to move. And instead of walking across the field to the portable bathrooms, he opted for a more efficient method of discharge, by relieving himself directly behind the Soccer net. As we were the last practice of the day, it was my responsibility to clean up the field and lock the storage sheds. Emotionally and mentally exhausted, I walked through the now empty fields and vacant parking lot, the mud and slime still squishing between my toes. Sitting by himself on the bench, almost peaceful and reflective, sat Johnny wondering and perhaps more hoping, that his Mother didn't forget him yet again. Johnny and I sat for nearly an hour before simple Sue's boyfriend showed up on his muffler-less motorcycle. Something's very wrong I tell you! Something's very wrong!

HAVE YOU MET WOODY ENHARD?

Something's very wrong I tell you! Something's very wrong! My name is Woody Enhard and I am a gymnasium bleacher. That's right. The same bleachers that you sit on every day to watch your clumsy, disoriented, high spirited, offspring, entertain you in their athletic endeavors. Every parent and student's nightmares have now come true, because I can talk. The things I have heard and seen will rock your world. The secrets that I am privy too will stun you. The backstabbing I have witnessed will crush you. I find it ironic that these pinhead parents talk through the same part of their anatomy that I unfortunately come into physical contact with every day! In case you haven't guessed, my job stinks! And there is not much to look up to either!

First of all, keep in mind that I am a genetic, wooden anomaly. Not all bleachers can talk especially those skanky, aluminum, low class bleachers. I am simply one of a kind. Experts have proven beyond any doubt that my unique ability to communicate is predicated on the very firm, natural grain of my wood, stressed by years and years of lunatic parents going against the grain! If you are sensing lots of bitterness in my voice, well, that would be an understatement. Look! Ninety percent of the families that shove their butts on top of me are actually quite nice, and their kids aren't bad either. Good families, teaching their kids good things. I'm talking about the ten percent. The minority. I'm talking about the family who lives across town. I'm talking about the Ass family –Smart Ass, Dumb Ass, Wise Ass and Sorry Ass.

Meet Smart Ass. He's the Dad. He claims to know every thing about every sport. In his simple mind, he missed his true calling in life and feels as though he should be the Head Coach of the next Superbowl contender. He shoves his machismo in your face on every occasion. (Hey, it could be worst. Think about what he shoves in mine). His testosterone flairs like an out of control forest fire when he is challenged by another dad on sports trivia. When I hear him speak to other dads, he's demeaning, derogatory and overpowering. He embellishes and generally, just outright lies about his son's athletic accomplishments, awards and game winning points. He pushes his athletic son well beyond every emotional and mentally healthy barrier – while remaining oblivious to the impact on his victimized child.

Meet Dumb Ass. She's the Mom. Actually, she's far from dumb. She's got an advanced college degree. She holds a white collar, well paid professional job and is highly respected by her peers. She sits on top of me for most of the games, clueless of what is happening on the field, while taking business phone calls and sending emails through her handheld device. But where the hell is she when it comes to protecting her son? Why can't she see what every neighbor, relative and other parent sees? Why can't she see what her husband is doing to her son? When I hear her speak to other moms, she says she *"wishes Smart Ass wouldn't push him so hard"*. She wishes Smart Ass *"would just let him have some fun at the games"*. She wishes Smart Ass would *"let him get involved with other friends and things outside of organized sports"*. Well Dumb Ass, it's up to you to make that happen. If he was beating your son with his fist, instead of pummeling his brain with words, would you do something then? C'mon Dumb Ass! Wake up!

Meet Wise Ass. He's the 'other son'. He's the son Mom and Dad don't talk about too often. He's not in any organized sport and has absolutely no desire to join one. He tried sports when he was younger. He liked it, and was actually pretty good, but he quit and quit firmly, despite the pushing and shoving of his dad. Obviously, this is a child robust with strong instincts and wisdom. He doesn't talk about sports and he doesn't care much about them. He manages above average grades. He hangs with a good circle of other kids. He likes girls, video games and skateboarding. He likes to hang out at the mall with his friends. He thinks someday he'd like to be a fireman. When I hear him speak to his friends, he says solemnly, *"I don't really see my Mom and Dad a lot. Sometimes I'd like to hang with them. But the only way that could happen is if I went to more of my brother's sports things – and that's boring sometimes, and there's a million people there."*.

Meet Sorry Ass. A hard working kid. An above average athlete. A kid who's complacent on the outside and sad on the inside. A kid who knows no other way to gain his Dad's love, than to earn it through sports. Something's very wrong I tell you. Something's very wrong!

AMPLIFY

Something's very wrong I tell you! Something's very wrong! National Congressman and U.S. Presidents need to stop ruining my kids sporting events. They appear at nearly every game. Unwelcome, un-invited and extremely irritating. Okay, while they may not be there physically, they are certainly there through the bad lessons that they teach our youth. Election after election, the winner of these political competitions spend most of his/her campaign defiling their competitors with untruths, and disgracing the most recognized, powerful, jobs in the world with slander, false allegations and embellishments. If it's acceptable for adults to publicly trample the most influential offices in the Land, then it must be acceptable for our children to sully the character and reputation of those authoritative figures in their lives? Maybe that explains why many of us are not too surprised when we witness a child loudly and publicly belittle a game referee on the field, rink or court. These are lessons taught by the most influential teachers in any child's life – Mom and Dad.

What are these egghead parents doing? What are they teaching our children? And why do we, the normal parents, sit back and do nothing about it? Game after game, we let the moronic mom or dad stand tall slinging insult after insult at the referees, who by all accounts are there to keep the children safe. Allowing and all too frequently encouraging our kids to learn from these examples is simply mindless. Have you ever known any amateur or professional referee to change his/her mind just because some parent launched a nutty all over him? This behavior is completely irrelevant. Totally irrelevant!

And if you try to explain this irrelevance to the fool of a parent, he'll rationalize his behavior with comments like: *"Well, I got caught up in the moment!"* Or, *"Why should we be the victim of a bad call from the ref?"* Or, *"That could cost us the game!"* Well Dimwit? As you amplify your voice in an attempt to gain support for your cause, try to follow along and watch me A-M-P-L-I-F-Y mine!

A – Authority. I want my child to respect those in authority. Teachers, bosses, coaches, police officers and so many more deserve that simple gesture.

M – Mistakes. I want my child to know that everyone makes mistakes. Referees included. I don't want him to grow up in fear that a mistake in his life will result in someone else publicly ridiculing him. I also don't want him growing up in fear that reaching a position of authority is a bad thing!

P – Public. I want my child to know that public humiliation of any other human being for any reason is completely unacceptable. Period.

L – Lose. I want my child to know that losing a game or competition is his responsibility to accept – just as winning is his privilege to enjoy. Blaming that loss on someone or something else is cowardly.

I – In Control. I want my child to know that life will toss him losses and that what is most important is how he/she maintains control and manages through those losses. You see fool? Screaming at that Referee accomplishes only one thing – it makes you, and only you look like an out-of-control ass!

F – Fun. I want my child to know that the odds of him/her being a professional athlete are pretty slim and that it is so much more important that he/she simply have fun with organized sports.

Y – You. I want my child to know that you, and all the card carrying morons in your club, are the anomaly. I want my child to know that your behavior is viewed by the vast majority as just plain ignorant. Something's very wrong I tell you! Something's very wrong!

I Failed! I Failed Miserably!

Something's very wrong I tell you! Something's very wrong! Today I did something - something wrong that I am not particularly proud of and immensely embarrassed by. I found myself overcome with emotion. An emotion that I regrettably acted on. An emotion that I could not control despite my complete awareness and my overwhelming desires to suppress it. I violated my true beliefs. I humiliated my spouse and my soul mate. And most importantly, I angered my youngest son to a point where he would not speak with me for the rest of the day. In his tiny, fourteen years of life, my son – my buddy – my pal - had never been so upset with me. Today, I became one of THEM. One of those parents I write about. One of those parents I chide. What was I thinking?

It was championship weekend. Our little town team had made it to the semi-finals. If we won this game, as we did the two prior, then tomorrow we would have a date with destiny and quite possibly be able to take home the title of State Champs. The air was electric. The music was pounding in the background. The sun was brighter and the sky was bluer. The kids, coaches and parents were on a natural high. Yesterday, we surprisingly beat some of the more powerful rivals who were favored to win it all. While many adults wondered how we had made it this far with only an average season behind us, others were insisting we deserved to be there from the very start. Either way, the kids could have cared less about the adult bantering. They were only focused on their one passion in life. They just wanted to play. Just play!

It's the 'just play' stuff that got me in trouble. In the first two games my son and a few other kids received very little playing time. While many of his buddies were regularly out there exchanging high fives and accolades, he and a few others sat quietly with diffidence, red-faced again and again and again. That quiet state of sitting during this adrenaline-filled, ecstatic event was an injustice. Every one of these kids should be living in the moment and gasping for their next anxious breadth of excitement. But instead that ridiculously quiet state of sitting mercilessly ate away at my heart slowly, painfully, one miserable bite at a time. If this was slowly sucking every ounce of life out of me, then what devastating impact could it possibly be having on my son? How was he feeling? I needed to hold his heart in my warm, bare hands and help him through this. I needed to help him breath. I needed to do this quickly. I needed to be assured that he played in tomorrow's Championship game as he and every other child on that team so righteously deserved to! This was my obligation as his father!

I could no longer restrain myself and I approached the coach a couple of hours before the big game. Might have my timing been better? Perhaps. But if I witnessed an adult physically abusing my son or any other child, should I wait till the beating is complete? If one of his teachers was consistently humiliating him in front of the entire classroom, should I wait for the semester to finish before approaching the teacher? Then why wait now! In my eyes, any type of abuse enacted by an adult on a child is ridiculous – physical, emotional or social abuse? As far as I'm concerned, the timing was perfect.

I caught up with the coach privately and asked him if he wanted *"my son to dress for the upcoming game"*. Before he could respond, I finished with *"because he certainly hasn't had a need to in the first couple of games.".* The response I received was stunning—*"I'm trying to win a championship game here and you're bothering me with this type of stuff?".* The fire in my belly exploded into a ball of white flames! *"I want to win too."* I retorted. *"But not at the expense of ANY one child on this team,!".* With no response and a synchronized wave of his hands he began to walk away. With one last burst I marched forward with, *"So win at any cost? Any cost? Is that what you're teaching the kids now?".* With his eyes bulging and his face turning shiny apple red, I continued with *"Coach. Go into that locker room right now and ask anyone of those kids – anyone of them - if they would rather (possibly) win the championship but have to sit on the bench to do it – or (possibly) lose the championship but be able to play the game. How do you think they're going to answer coach? Huh? Stop confusing what you want with what the kids want?".* Angered and neutralized, he turned and quickly walked away from me. His anger was overshadowed only by his frustration of not being able to intelligently respond!

And just when I thought my angst could certainly not be eclipsed, I was soon to find out that the coach had shared my 'man to man' conversation with my child in the locker room, along with the rest of the team – leaving me to deal with a bewildered and embarrassed son. I guess I can no longer say that *"I never met a coach I didn't respect".* I still have no idea what emotion compelled this coach to share this private, adult conversation with the children? I also have no idea what emotions drove me to take the actions that I did. And while I feel terrible about confronting any one of these 'usually terrific', volunteer coaches, at the same time I offer no regrets at all about initiating it. That day, I just wanted to stand on top of the tallest building and scream out loud to anyone who would listen to me. *"Adults, wake up! Please! We have lost complete perspective!! Is winning some stupid game more important than how we play that game? Is winning more important than crushing a child's self esteem? Is winning more important than what they learn from their adult role models? It's just a stupid game! It's just a stupid game!* Something's very wrong I tell you! Something's very wrong!

HEY FOOL? IT'S ME!

Something's very wrong I tell you! Something's very wrong! You're full of it fool. Ain't nothing wrong here, just something wrong with you. That's all. I'm THAT dad. I'm that dad you've been writing about. That dad who supposedly pushes his kid too hard. That dad who supposedly doesn't love his kid. That dad who only thinks about sports. Well, I'm here to tell you that you are way off base here. You have no right to say these things. You say all this stuff about me because you don't understand. You don't understand what it takes to get to the next level. What it takes to reach a goal. What it takes to develop discipline. You don't understand that these lessons that kids learn in sports are lessons that will be helpful to them in life, in the workplace. Sure I push my kid. I push him very hard. If I don't then no one else will. And he'll fail. And he'll end up always looking over his shoulder saying *"if only, if only, if only"*. He'll never be happy.

So you say that I don't love him. But that's just plain wrong. Of course I love him. Just yesterday, he had an incredible game. He was flawless offensively and defensively. He couldn't do anything wrong. Even after the game, I overheard the other parents talking about how well he played. The coach mentioned something to him in the locker room. Even one of the dad's who I don't get along with very well, saw my son after the game and told him he played his best game ever. When we got into the car, I was exploding with excitement. We talked about the game the entire ride home. When we got to the top of the driveway, I told him how proud I was of him and that I loved him.

So you say that I force him to play against his own will. You don't know my son. He needs to be pushed. If he didn't he would sit on the sofa all day playing video games and eating Twinkies. I'm not going to let that happen to my son. Not like some of those other lazy parents do. You know? It's a lot of work for me too. I have to bring him to practices. I taxi him all over the place from game to game to game. We're up early on weekend mornings and out late during weekday nights. We never have enough time to have a quiet dinner or just chill out watching a good movie together. He doesn't hear me complaining though. I sacrifice all my down time for his activities. I give it all up so he can be happy. I go without so he goes with. I know he understands this because when I explain it to him, he nods his head. I've asked him on a few occasions if he felt like quitting. I gave him his chance. I told him while I would be disappointed, I'd allow it. I gave him his chance.

So you say that I coach too much from the sidelines. You say that I need to be more positive, more encouraging instead of pointing out all the things he does wrong. Look. He can't pick his coaches and neither can I. He's had a bad streak of pretty lousy coaches lately. Just because they don't know what they are doing out there doesn't mean that my kid should suffer. Some of these guys don't care about winning or losing. What type of lesson is that? I want my kid to learn winning. Period. Most of these coaches don't even understand the game. They think because they were some flunkie who played in high school twenty five years ago that they are qualified to coach my kid. I'm not gonna let them teach my kid the wrong things out there. If I tick off a coach or two then that's just too bad.

So you say I embarrass my kid in front of his friends when I'm on the bleachers yelling at him after he does something wrong.

Hey. It's a tough world out there. My boss yells at me when I do something wrong and I don't see him apologizing. My wife yells at me for not putting down the toilet seat cover. The cop yells at me when I try to tell him again and again that he just didn't see me come to a full stop at the stop sign. The Doctor yells at me for not taking my medications. Look. We live in a world where everyone yells at you. He's got to suck it up and learn that now. He shouldn't be embarrassed in front of his friends. I'm sure they all get yelled at later, when they get home.

So you say I'm teaching him that all referees and umpires suck. Well? Hello?

So you say my kid isn't as good an athlete as I think he is. That I somehow think he's better than everyone else sees him. Let me tell you. I've been around sports my whole life. Sure, my kid still has a lot to learn. But he's got a couple of things none of these other kids got. He's got discipline. He's got ambition. He's got desire. He can get a full college scholarship if he applies himself now. He can play Pro if he really wants it bad enough. Like some famous guy said once *"it's 10% perspiration and 90% inspiration"*. Well he's got all that right stuff. I work on that with him. I remind him all the time, sometimes every day, how bad he wants to be an athlete.

So you say I'm living out my sports fantasies through my son's eyes. Unlike some of these clueless coaches I've had to deal with, I am a real athlete. Hey, it's not my fault that I blew out my knee senior year in high school. If I hadn't I definitely could have gone onto college with a full boat and most likely, played Pro. My life would be big time different right now if it wasn't for that dam injury. I'd be happy right now and my family would be happy. Don't get me wrong. I guess I'm happy now, but things would just be a lot different. My dad pushed me hard and I sure turned out okay. So of course I'm gonna push my kid hard too. And there ain't nothing wrong with that no matter how many times you say that "Something's very wrong I tell you. Something's very wrong!".

Mom? Dad? Can We Talk?

Hi Mom. Hi Dad. I think something's wrong. I think something's very wrong. That's why I'm writing you this letter. I've tried to talk to you before about this stuff, but you always end up yelling. Then I feel bad. Then after that I feel really angry. So I thought that maybe if I wrote you a letter then I would be able to say everything that I want to without you interrupting me. Don't throw this letter out until you are done reading it okay? And please don't yell at me again after you read it okay?

I love you guys so much. And I know you do a lot for me and Sis. You spend a lot of money even when you probably don't have a lot. I know you guys don't buy stuff for yourself so you can buy stuff for us. And I know that you teach us things so we don't get hurt like you guys did growing up. And I know that you love Sis and me more than anything. And I see how some of my best friend's parents are and how they don't do much with their kids. Sis and I are lucky and we know that.

Dad, I've been playing baseball with you ever since I was like three or four years old or something like that. It's been forever. It was fun. I liked playing catch with you in the front yard. You would teach me. And then we would talk a lot about things when we took water breaks. And I liked it when you coached my teams for a little bit. But I liked it more when we just played catch in the front yard. Sometimes when you were coaching, or sometimes after that when you were just watching the games like the other parents, I would get angry with you. I would still love you. But I would get very angry at you when you would tell me how to throw or catch or run or bat the ball. I know how to do all that stuff because I've been doing it my whole life. And when you yell at me like that in front of all the other parents and all of my friends, sometimes I don't even know what you're saying because I get too angry at you to hear it.

I really try hard when I'm on the field Dad. Honest. All the other kids think I'm one of the best players on the team. And the coaches tell me I do really, really well too. And when coach tells me to fix something I'm doing wrong, he tells me nicely. I hear him when he tells me. One time Dad, I heard my two coaches talking about you and I didn't like what they were saying. They didn't know I was listening. I was so angry at them for what they were saying. I didn't want to tell you because it was mean and I thought you might cry or feel hurt so I just didn't say anything to even my best friends. That was when I quit the Baseball team. I didn't want to go back ever, but you made me. Another time when I was in the dugout, one of the kids starting saying that you were always yelling bad things at the whole team and telling us what we did wrong. Because you always yelled mean things to the team and umpires and never good things, you were mean. That's why I got into a fight with that boy that day. And that's why I quit the baseball team again. I didn't want to go back ever, but you made me.

I know that you like me to be on a lot of different baseball teams Dad and you think it's going to make me a better player. But sometimes I like to do other stuff too. I really wanted to tryout for the school soccer team because it looks like a lot of fun. And I kind of like this girl too Dad. She's wicked nice and pretty. I thought we were going out once, but she said that she didn't want to because I was always at baseball practices and games. And she didn't like baseball too much. And most of all, sometimes I really want to just hang out with my friends after school. Like go over someone's house to play video games or something. Or maybe just go to the mall to hang out and stuff. But I can never do those things because I have practice or a game. And then finally, when I don't have baseball stuff and I can go somewhere, I don't get invited.

I know that my homework is easy for you because your old and stuff, but it's still pretty hard for me. Sometimes when I'm at school all day and at practice all night and then I have to come home and shower because I stink and then eat dinner all by myself, well, by then I don't feel like doing homework sometimes. I'm tired. And maybe that's why I don't get good grades all the time. I'm really trying hard to do everything that you want me to do and I'm trying to do my best like you tell me all the time.

But Dad, I'm really sorry and all, because I know baseball is so important to you. But I think I don't like baseball that much anymore. I don't even feel like trying hard sometimes when I'm in the field. I liked it more when it was fun and we didn't have to win every single game. I liked it when it was just for fun. I liked it the most when you and I would just play catch in the front yard and talk and stuff. I love you Dad, but something's very wrong I tell you! Something's very wrong!

EPILOGUE

So there you have it. Now what do we do? How do we make it better? It beats the hell out of me. I guess we'll have to let all those experts figure that out. I think at the end of the day, each of us is only capable of controlling our own individual environments and ensuring that our own children are learning the right things. I've always viewed the behavior of these bumbling parents as a cancer. They need a host to survive. If we don't provide the host – if we don't serve as their listening board – if we show our disapproval – if we simply walk away when they begin their tirades – then maybe just maybe, the cancer stops growing *(even though I'm not a doctor, I think my mom would be very proud of that analogy!)*.

From the first day my kids began with sports we've always practiced the same conversation on the ride home. I nicknamed the conversation S-E-L-F. We didn't rehash every detail of the game. We didn't talk about the final score. We didn't talk about the errors. We didn't talk about the bad call from the ref. What we did talk about were the same four things after every game.

- We talked about 'S' – Skill. I focused only on the positive of any one skill. We didn't talk about the three times she struck out that game. We talked about the one time she ran really fast to stop the ball that rolled between her legs into right field.
- We talked about 'E' – Effort. This one always sounded the same. *"Did you try your hardest out there today?"* And the answer was always *"Yes Dad."* And always the same retort *"Well then, nothing else matters son."* Even if they fibbed and didn't try their hardest - they understood.

- We talked about '<u>L</u>' – Learn. *"What did you learn today?"* And sometimes the only thing he learned was that his friend on the other team has a sister who thinks he's cute. But that's okay. We talked about that all the way home.
- We talked about '<u>F</u>' – Fun. We focused on one fun thing that happened during warm-ups, at the game or in the locker room, and we laughed all over again, together.

Perhaps the best solution to return the enjoyment back to the children and to the games is the simplest and cheapest solution. Let's each spend a few dollars, buy a can of paint, a brush, a few nails and an old piece of scrap plywood. In the middle of the plywood, we place a big, shiny mirror. And at the entrance of every sports field, court, rink and track in the country, we post a sign that simply says *"Want to improve youth sports? Look here".*

So what do you think is wrong?

Visit SomethingsVeryWrong.com and tell us!

www.SomethingsVeryWrong.com

Keep watching for Tom's second book

in the **'Something's Very Wrong'** series

titled

"Customer Service Has Left the Building".

Available in 2009

Visit

www.SomethingsVeryWrong.com

ABOUT THE AUTHOR

Tom is the proud father of three children, Lindsey, Tommy and Alex; and an enamored husband to his wife, Diane of 23 years. They have spent their entire lives in the convenient and friendly town of Salem, New Hampshire. Tom is a dedicated and supportive dad to all of his children's extracurricular activities. He is often recognized as the thunderous and boisterous cheerleader who bellows positive encouragements to all of the children. While nothing exhilarates Tom more than attending one of his children's events; nothing agitates him more than the misfit, sports parent who demonstrates complete disregard for everyone else. Over the years, Tom's humorous writings of these unapologetic parents have served as an effective form of self-therapy for Tom; while thoroughly entertaining all who read them.